Storywriter

Y3/P4

Kate Ruttle

Series Consultant: Pie Corbett

OXFORD

UNIVERSITY PRESS

Contents

Write a story set in places you know.

Stories with familiar settings — 4

What are stories with familiar settings? — 4
Author interview — 6
Reading as a writer — 8
Planning to write your story — 10
Writing your story — 13
Improving your story — 14
Publishing your story — 17

Traditional tales — 18

What are traditional tales? — 18
Author interview — 20
Reading as a writer — 22
Planning to write your story — 24
Writing your story — 27
Improving your story — 28
Publishing your story — 31

Once upon a time, a very long time ago …

Are you ready for the excitement...?

Adventure stories   32

What are adventure stories?   32
Author interview   34
Reading as a writer   36
Planning to write your story   38
Writing your story   41
Improving your story   42
Publishing your story   45

WRITER'S TOOL KIT    46

Creating a character   47
Creating a setting   50
Paragraphs for planning   52
Story connectives bank   53
Punctuation   54
Story writer's glossary   56

Use the Writer's Tool Kit to help you with the nuts and bolts of writing!

Stories with familiar settings

What are stories with familiar settings?

Stories in familiar settings are set in real places and are about 'real life' people, their feelings and the things they do.

Places you know well could be:

Exciting places

◎ an old house

◎ the football ground

◎ a strip of wasteland

◎ an old tin mine

Secret places

◎ a tree house

◎ a den by an old wall

◎ behind the shed

◎ a place under some overgrown bushes

Ordinary places

◎ a playground

◎ a park

◎ a shopping centre

◎ your home

Holiday places

◎ an old castle

◎ cliffs by the sea

◎ underground caves

◎ a forest

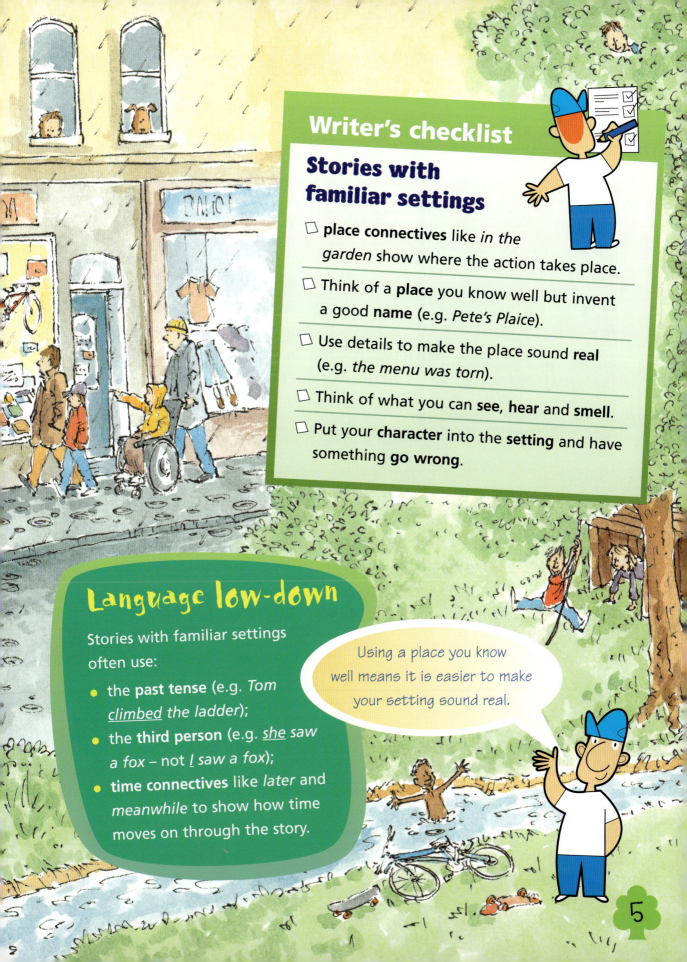

Writer's checklist

Stories with familiar settings

☐ **place connectives** like *in the garden* show where the action takes place.

☐ Think of a **place** you know well but invent a good **name** (e.g. *Pete's Plaice*).

☐ Use details to make the place sound **real** (e.g. *the menu was torn*).

☐ Think of what you can **see**, **hear** and **smell**.

☐ Put your **character** into the **setting** and have something **go wrong**.

Language low-down

Stories with familiar settings often use:

- the **past tense** (e.g. *Tom* <u>*climbed*</u> *the ladder*);
- the **third person** (e.g. <u>*she*</u> *saw a fox* – not <u>*I*</u> *saw a fox*);
- **time connectives** like *later* and *meanwhile* to show how time moves on through the story.

> Using a place you know well means it is easier to make your setting sound real.

Author interview

Chris Powling

Here I am, standing in front of a very special shelf in my workroom. On this, I keep all my stuff about Charlton Athletic - the football team I've supported all my life. For me, being a writer is the best job in the world. For second-best, though, I'd choose being a Charlton striker...

Where do you get your ideas?

From anywhere and everywhere. An idea can come from something you see, something somebody says, something that just pops into your head without any warning. I've trained myself to jot down this 'something' in a notebook in case I forget it.

How do you use the settings you know?

The lovely thing about familiar settings is that they are just that – familiar. You're surrounded by them – where you live, where you play, where you go to school. You've already got all the details you need.

6

How do you make the settings sound real?

Never tell the reader too much. For a start, this will be boring – like reading a list. Also, it'll stop the reader using their own experience, seeing their own setting in their head. That's what you want to plug into.

What do you focus on when you write?

Mostly, I try to focus on what gets the readers 'hooked' so they can't bear to put the story down. That's the most important and difficult trick in all storytelling: to describe what's happening right now in a way that sets up what happens next.

What do you do after you've written your draft?

I go back over it to look for ways to make it better. Funnier, perhaps. Or more vivid. Or more exciting. Or to see if I can improve the pace. (Pace means the speed with which things happen on the page.) If readers get to the most important bit of the story too quickly you'll have lost your chance to hook them. If the story is too slow, though, readers won't even get as far as the important bit.

What are your top tips for writers of stories with familiar settings?

A top tip to get ideas for your story with a familiar setting is to use your own memories – about your happiest time, or saddest time, or funniest time, for instance.

But my number one top tip for becoming a writer of stories with familiar settings is to READ stories with familiar settings. Do this and you're bound to succeed.

Reading as a writer

Opening

● Introduces the reader to time, setting and main character(s). Shows how the main character feels and makes the reader want to read on.

Build-up

● Sets the scene for what is going to happen in the climax.

Climax

● The exciting bit of the story – the main action of the story as the main character(s) tackle(s) the task.

Resolution

● This is the end of the climax – the main character gets out of the difficult situation.

Ending

● Wraps up the story neatly.
● Often ties in closely to the opening.

1 Read as a writer → **2** Make a plan → **3** Write

New Boy

Sam stared across the playground. It was his first day at Pollbrook Primary. He wanted to go back to his old school where all his friends were, but he and his mum had moved house. This was his school now. He watched a group of children kicking a tennis ball around. Plucking up his courage, he went over to them.

"Can I play?" he muttered.

"No way!" snapped a tall girl.

All the children laughed. Sam turned away, trying to hide his tears. He wandered over to a bench and sat down.

A few minutes later a boy came and sat on the bench beside Sam. After a while, the boy asked, "Do you like football?"

"Yes," Sam replied. "I was on the team in my old school. I was the Captain because I'm fast."

The boy looked at him. "Well, we need you on our team then," he said. "Our team is useless. We always lose."

That afternoon, Sam stood on his own and watched the school football team playing a match. They really were useless. They were five nil down. Miss Long had said that he could be a reserve, but he probably wouldn't get to play.

Suddenly, the tall girl who had been mean to Sam that morning let out a scream. She'd been stung by a wasp. Miss Long sighed and glanced at Sam.

"Well, we're going to lose anyway," she said, "so you might as well have a go."

Sam ran onto the field. The children in the team ignored him. When the game started again, the ball never seemed to come near him. But then, Sam tackled the other team's Captain. Skilfully, he dribbled the ball up the pitch towards the goal. He dodged round one defender, then two. Now there was only the goalie. He blasted the ball into the back of the net. There was a stunned silence, then he heard a cheer.

When the final whistle went the score was five all.

"Well," said Miss Long. "That's the best score we've ever had. When we replay St Bart's next week, you'll be in the team Sam."

Sam grinned. Perhaps Pollbrook Primary wouldn't be so bad after all.

Planning to write your story

Where is your story set?

For your setting, choose a place you know well.

Has your setting got a **name**? (E.g. Big Dip, Snailwell, Fred's Den?)

What is the **weather** like? (E.g. sunny, stormy, windy?)

What **time of day/year** is it? (E.g. early morning in the summer; night-time on Christmas Eve; a Sunday afternoon?)

What can you **see** and **hear**? (E.g. rush hour traffic, school bell, animals?)

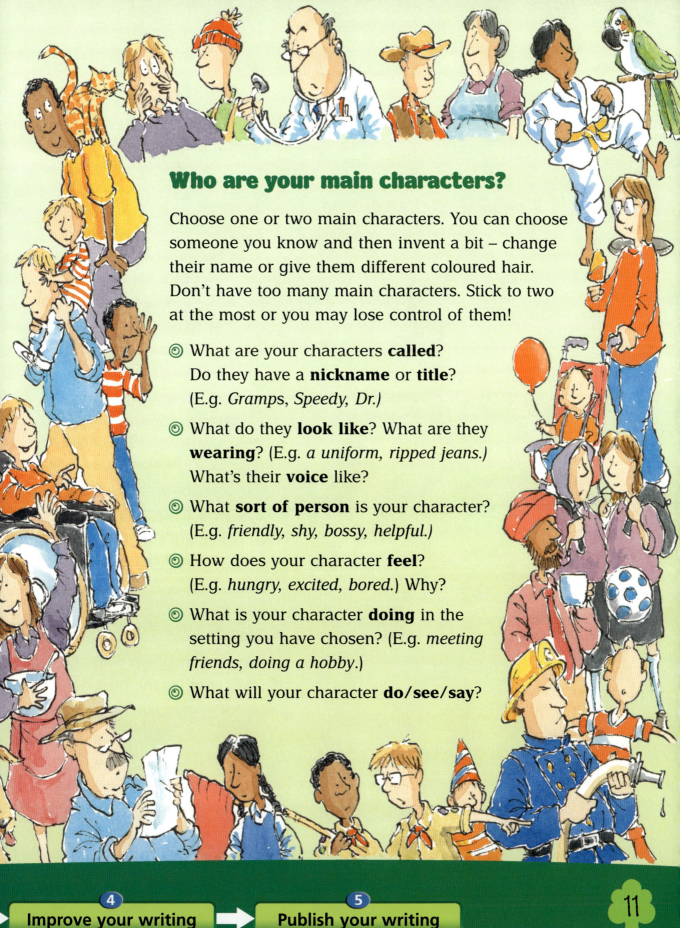

Who are your main characters?

Choose one or two main characters. You can choose someone you know and then invent a bit – change their name or give them different coloured hair. Don't have too many main characters. Stick to two at the most or you may lose control of them!

◎ What are your characters **called**? Do they have a **nickname** or **title**? (E.g. *Gramps, Speedy, Dr.*)

◎ What do they **look like**? What are they **wearing**? (E.g. *a uniform, ripped jeans.*) What's their **voice** like?

◎ What **sort of person** is your character? (E.g. *friendly, shy, bossy, helpful.*)

◎ How does your character **feel**? (E.g. *hungry, excited, bored.*) Why?

◎ What is your character **doing** in the setting you have chosen? (E.g. *meeting friends, doing a hobby.*)

◎ What will your character **do/see/say**?

Planning to write your story

What is your story about?

◎ Your main character finds or loses something special?

◎ An unfriendly character becomes friendly?

◎ Someone gets into trouble?

◎ Someone plays a trick?

Make a story map

The boys and girls won't let Sam play.

A boy sits beside Sam and says the football team is useless.

Sam watches the match. The tall girl is stung. Sam plays and scores.

The teams draw. Sam is in the team for the next time.

Sam feels better.

Writing your story

tall girl with long hair →

Sam ↓

Miss Long

Wasp

Sam ↘

Team

- Practise your story by telling it aloud.
- Use your planning grid or story map to help you to remember what happened when.
- Jot down useful words and phrases on your planning grid.

Top tips for writing

- Try to **see the setting** in your mind.
- Begin with the main characters doing **something they enjoy**.
- Have something **go wrong** (e.g. *a shout for help; a bully appears; someone gets lost*).
- Use **powerful verbs** and **nouns** (e.g. *the caretaker bellowed,* not *the man shouted*).
- Describe what characters **hear/see/smell/touch/taste**.
- Tell your reader about the characters' **thoughts** and **feelings**.
- Make sure that there is a **reason** for all of the events in the story.

Improving your story

How would you **improve** this story? Can you find the **mistakes**?

Ways to improve

- Don't use too many 'ands' – use full stops or a different connective instead.
- Use more powerful verbs.
- Make sure you show who is speaking by using speech marks and layout.
- Join short sentences with some interesting connectives.

Mistakes

- Careless spelling
- Missing capital letters, full stops and question marks
- Paragraphs not used properly
- Missing speech marks
- Wrong tense used

Anything else?

Now do the *Writer's Mumble*.
Read your story aloud to yourself.
- Does your story create a picture of the place you know well?
- Check the language – is it right for your audience?
- Is there anything you need to change?
- Have you rushed the ending?

1 Read as a writer

2 Make a plan

3 Write

New Boy

Sam looked across the playground and it was his first day at Pollbrook Primary and he watched a group of children kicking a ball around and he went over to them. Can I play he said. no way she said and all the children laughed then he went to a bench and sat down.

a boy came and sat on the bench beside him. Then he said do you like football Yes I was on the team in my old school. I was the Captain because I'm fast. Well, we need you on our team cos our team is useless and we always lose.

Sam looked at the school football team playing a match. They really were really useless. They are five nil down. Miss Long said that he could be a reserve, but he probably wouldn't get to play. Suddenly, the tall girl who had been mean to Sam that morning let out a scream. She'd been stung by a wasp. Miss Long sighed and looked at Sam. Well, we're going to lose anyway so you might as well have a go. Sam runs onto the field. When the game starts again, the ball never comes near. But then Sam tackles the other team's Captain and he dribbles the ball up the pitch towards the goal he dodges round one defender and he dodges round he next one and now there's only the goalie then he kicks the ball into the back of the net and there's a stunned silence then he hears a cheer.

When the final whistle went the score was five all. Miss Long said that's the best score we've ever had and when we replay St Bart's next week, you'll be in the team Sam.

Sam grinned. Perhaps Pollbrook Primary wouldn't be so bad after all.

Improving your story

Make it better!

Try to improve your own story by:

- ♣ including **descriptions** (e.g. *the sun blazed and a hawk hovered in the blue sky* not *it was a lovely day*);
- ♣ using **careful nouns** instead of a noun and an adjective (e.g. *the Ferrari* not *the expensive car*);
- ♣ using **paragraphs** for each part of the story;
- ♣ not rushing the **ending**.

Language check

Have you used:

- ♣ the **past tense** all the way through?
- ♣ **third person pronouns** (e.g. *he, she, they*) except in dialogue?
- ♣ **time connectives** to tie the story together (e.g. *once, when, while, after*)?
- ♣ **place connectives** to show where things happen/characters are (e.g. *in the park; on the swings*)?

Oops! Things to check for

- ♣ Sentence punctuation
- ♣ Speech marks if you have used speech
- ♣ Missing words (it's easy to miss out *the* and *a)*
- ♣ Spelling

important words in the story (e.g. *friend, classroom*)

common words (e.g. *they, because, with*)

ing and *ed* words (e.g. *moving, hopped*)

Publishing your story

Remember who your story is for.

How are you going to share your story?

tell it

put it on a website

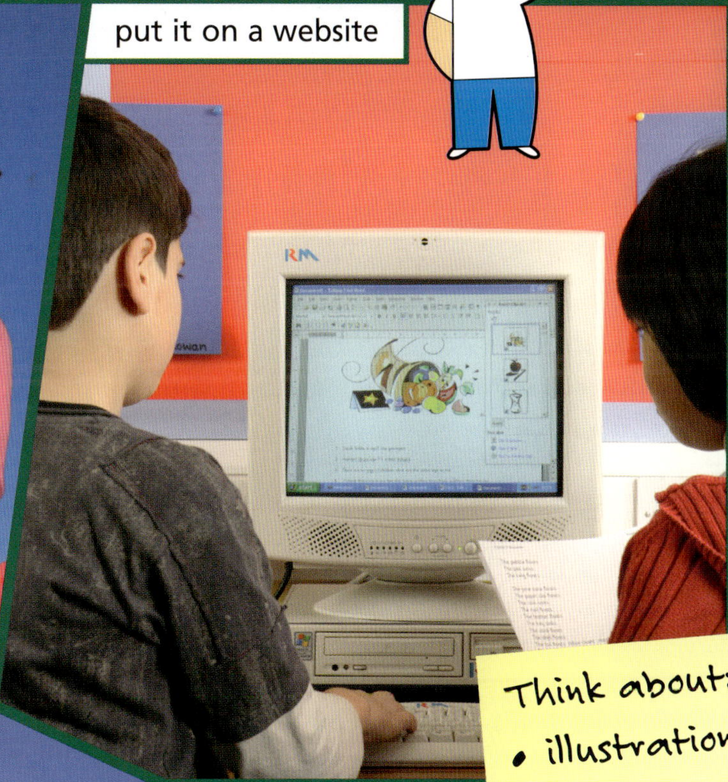

display it

FAMILIAR SETTINGS

make a book

Think about:
• illustrations
• blurb
• cover

Traditional tales

What are traditional tales?

Before there were any books, stories were told. Every evening people would gather round the fire and someone would begin a story. Storytellers travelled from village to village telling tales. In this way, stories travelled.

These stories are now written down and are known as traditional tales.

Types of traditional tales

◎ **Fairy tales and folk tales** are stories that are often told to children. Many contain magic and animals that can speak. Examples are *Anansi*, *Cinderella* and *The Three Bears*.

◎ **Myths** are stories which are told to explain how or why something happens. Examples are *How the Moon Appeared* and *Why the Cat Lands on its Feet*.

◎ **Legends** are about things that really happened in the past. People have added more exciting bits as the stories were retold. Most legends involve heroes and heroines. Examples are the legends of *Robin Hood* and *King Arthur*.

◎ **Fables** are usually short tales with a moral. The main characters are often creatures who can speak. Examples are *Aesop's Fables*.

Writer's checklist

Traditional tales

☐ Use '**runs**' where you repeat a phrase (e.g. *He walked and he walked and he walked*).

☐ Often use the **rule of three** (e.g. *three bears, three tasks*).

☐ Have **stock characters** (e.g. *the unhappy princess, the third child*).

☐ Use **stock settings** (e.g. *forest, lonely tower, tumbledown cottage*).

Language low-down

Traditional tales are usually written:

- with **traditional beginnings** and **endings** (e.g. *Once upon a time…*, *And they lived happily ever after*);
- with some **patterned language** (e.g. *She tried the porridge in the first bowl, but … she tried the porridge in the second bowl, but …*);
- in the **past tense** (e.g. *Jack climbed the beanstalk*);
- in the **third person** (e.g. *he saw a giant* not *I saw a giant*);
- to **talk to the reader** (e.g. *And what do you think happened next?* or *Oh ho! She didn't like that!*);
- with **time connectives** like *three days later* and *meanwhile* to show when things happen;
- with **place connectives** like *in the forest* to show where the action takes place.

Author interview

Rosalind Kerven

I live in an old stone cottage in the wild hills of Northumberland. I am married with two daughters and a very beautiful rough-collie dog called Amber.

Why do you like retelling traditional tales?

Traditional tales are very, very old - like ancient treasures. I love thinking back through history and imagining all the thousands of people who have told these stories before me.

How do you choose which stories to retell?

My bookshelves are filled with collections of traditional tales from all over the world. From these I look for stories which are full of my favourite things: magic and adventure!

How do you retell a story?

I read one or more old versions of the tale very carefully and make step-by-step notes on the plot. I think carefully about what happens, the characters, and how I want to retell the story.

I write a first draft and print it out on my computer. I read through the draft, cross loads of it out, add things and change it around. It usually looks a complete mess!

I screw up my first draft and throw it away. Then I print out my new draft, read it aloud and make more changes. Some stories are easy to retell. But I revise others 20 or 30 times until I feel that every word is right!

How much do you change the tale?

I never change the basic plot, or the main characters. But I might make some of the characters younger or older, or add interesting details about them. Sometimes I move the plot around a bit to make it more exciting and meaningful.

What is your top tip for writers of traditional tales?

Imagine you are writing your story for a fierce king who has threatened to chop off your head unless your version is the best one he has ever heard!

21

Reading as a writer

Opening
- Introduces reader to time, setting and main character(s).
- Often sets up the problem or task.

Build-up
- Sets the scene for what is going to happen in the climax.
- Often sets up a pattern of words or events.

Climax
- The exciting bit of the story.

Resolution
- The problem is solved or the task completed.

Ending
- Wraps up the story neatly.
- Lessons learned/happy endings.

1 Read as a writer → **2** Make a plan → **3** Write

Tortoise Tug

Once upon a time, Tortoise was walking in the jungle when Elephant trod on her toe.

"Ouch!" cried Tortoise. "Look where you're going!"

"You're so small, I didn't see you," laughed Elephant.

"I may be small, but I'm strong!" Tortoise boasted. "Indeed, I'm so strong that I challenge you to a tug-of-war!"

Elephant laughed until he hiccupped, but agreed that he would be at the tallest tree at one o'clock the next day.

Tortoise walked on. Suddenly Hippo trod on her tail.

"Ouch!" cried Tortoise. "Look where you're going!"

"You're so small, I didn't even see you," laughed Hippo.

"I may be small, but I'm strong!" Tortoise boasted. "I'm so strong, indeed, that I challenge you to a tug-of-war."

Hippo howled with laughter but agreed that he would be at the widest tree at ten past one the next day.

At one o'clock the next day, Tortoise met Elephant at the tallest tree and showed him the end of a long rope.

"You're going to pull this end of the rope," she explained, "and I'm going to pull the other. You wait here until I shout 'Pull!', then you should pull. OK?"

Elephant wiped the tears from his eyes and nodded weakly.

At ten past one, Tortoise met Hippo at the widest tree. Tortoise showed him the other end of the rope and explained that he should wait until she shouted 'pull'. Hippo stopped giggling for long enough to nod.

Tortoise walked to a place between the two animals and shouted "PULL!" At once Elephant and Hippo both started pulling. They pulled and they pulled and they pulled until at last, they both gave the most mighty of pulls and fell flat onto the jungle floor!

As Elephant lay panting on his side, he saw Tortoise coming towards him, grinning from ear to ear.

"See?" she said, "I may be small but I'm strong. Now you must promise never to tread on me again. If you keep your promise, I won't tell the other animals that I won the tug-of-war."

"Oh thank you, Tortoise!" sobbed Elephant.

A few minutes later, Tortoise had the same conversation with Hippo.

And ever since then, hippos and elephants have been very careful not to tread on tortoises!

Planning to write your story

What is your story about?

Before you plan your traditional tale, decide whether you are going to write:

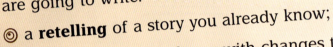

◎ a **retelling** of a story you already know;

◎ a story you already know with changes to:
  - **names and places** (e.g. *Once upon a time there was a girl called Vicky who went for a walk around a park. She had not been walking for long when she found a cottage belonging to three foxes*);
  - **characters** (e.g. *Once upon a time there were three good little wolves*);
  - the **setting** (e.g. *To get to the other side, the goats had to cross a busy motorway*);

◎ a **new** story of your own with traditional tales' themes and characters.

Themes for your story might be:

◎ **transformation** (e.g. *poor to rich, sad to happy, foolish to wise*);

◎ **a trick** (e.g. *Brer Rabbit stories, Anansi spider man stories*);

◎ **wishes** (e.g. *Cinderella, Three Wishes*);

◎ **a journey** in search of something important;

◎ **defeating a monster** (e.g. *Jack and the Beanstalk*);

◎ **an explanation** (if you're writing a myth, you will be explaining something);

◎ **a moral** (fables need morals at the end).

1 **Read as a writer** ➔ 2 **Make a plan** ➔ 3 **Write**

Who are your main characters?

◎ Who is your main character
(e.g. *giant, animal, little girl/boy*)?

◎ What is your main character like
(e.g. *brave, cowardly, wise*)?

◎ What will they have to do in the story?

◎ How do they change or what will they
learn by the end of the story (e.g.
*start off poor and become rich; learn
that it's not good to be greedy*)?

Planning to write your story

Where is your story set?

◎ Choose a stock setting (e.g. *forest, cottage, castle*).

◎ What details can you see (e.g. *tall trees, talking creatures, a waterfall*)?

◎ What details can you hear (e.g. *a dragon roar, giant footsteps, thundering, a mirror talking*)?

◎ What happens there?

Make a storyboard

Tortoise walking in jungle. Elephant treads on her toe.
Hippo treads on Tortoise's tail.
Tortoise sets up tug of war.
Elephant and Hippo pull and fall over.
Elephant and Hippo promise not to tread on Tortoise again.

1 Read as a writer → **2** Make a plan → **3** Write

Writing your story

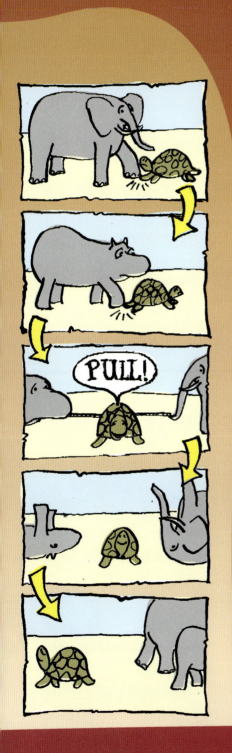

- Practise your story by telling it aloud.
- Use your planning grid or story board to help you to remember what happened when.
- Jot down useful words and phrases on your planning grid.

Top tips for writing

- Try telling a story that you **know well**, like the *Billy Goats Gruff*.
- Try to change it a bit by **altering** the **characters** and the **setting** (e.g. *the three snowmen have to cross the road*).
- **Change** a character (e.g. *the troll was trying to stop the goats from destroying the rare plants in the green meadow*).
- Use a **modern setting** (e.g. *Cinderella in a disco*).
- Use two or three **senses** in the climax to the story (e.g. *As she ran from the palace, she felt the cold of the marble stairs through the thin soles of her shoes*).
- Use the **rule of three** (e.g. *three wishes*).
- Make sure that there is a **reason** for all of the events in the story.

Improving your story

How would you **improve** this story? Can you find the **mistakes**?

Ways to improve

- Don't use too many 'ands' – use full stops or a different connective instead.
- Use more powerful verbs.
- Don't use too many adjectives – use fewer adjectives and better nouns.
- Use pronouns carefully.

Mistakes

- Careless spelling
- Missing capital letters, full stops and question marks
- Paragraphs not used properly
- Missing speech marks
- Wrong tense

Anything else?

Now do the *Writer's Mumble*.
Read your story aloud to yourself.
- Have you used stock characters and a stock setting?
- Check the language – is it right for your audience?
- Is there anything you need to change?
- Have you written a traditional ending?

Tortoise Tug

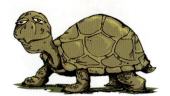

tortoise was going in the jungle then the big large elephant trod on her toe.

"ouch!" said tortoise. "look where i'm going!"

"you're so small, i didn't see you," said elephant.

"i'm small, but i'm nice!" tortoise said. i'm so nice that i want to have a tug-of-war with you."

elephant said yes.

tortoise went on then the big large hippo trod on her tails.

"ouch!" said tortoises. "look where you're going!"

"you're so small, i didn't see you," said hippo.

"i'm small, but i'm nice!"!" tortoise said. "i'm so nice that i want to have a tug-of-war with you."

hippo said yes.

Then tortoise met elephant and showed him the end of a long thick strong rope.

"you're going to pull this end of the long thick strong rope," she said, "and i'm going to pull the other end of the long thick strong rope. you wait here until i shout 'pull!',

Then tortoise met hippo and tortoise showed him the other end of the long thick strong rope and said that he should wait until she said 'pull'.

tortoise went to a place and said "pull!" and then elephant and hippo started pulling and then they both gave a big huge large massive pull and fell over

Tortoise went up to elephant and hippo

"I am nice and I won't tell anyone if you don't tread on me."

They both said OK

And hippos and elephants don't tread on tortoises.

Improving your story

Make it better!

Try to improve your own story by:

- using **powerful verbs** (e.g. *roared* not *said*; *stumbled* not *went*);
- including **descriptions** (e.g. *the dragon's dark lair was surrounded by thorns* rather than *there was a cave*);
- using **questions** to talk to the reader;
- using **paragraphs** for each part of the story.

Language check

Have you used:

- **traditional language** (e.g. *once upon a time*)?
- the **past tense** all the way through?
- **third person pronouns** (e.g. *he, she, they*) except in dialogue?
- **time connectives** to tie the story together (e.g. *once, when, while after*)?
- **place connectives** to show where things happen (e.g. *in the cave; under the bridge*)?
- **full stops** and **capital letters**?
- **speech marks** if you have used speech?

Oops! Things to check for

- Punctuation, and speech marks if you have used speech
- Missing words (it's easy to miss out *the* and *a)*
- Spelling

common words (e.g. *they, because, with*)

ing and *ed* words (e.g. *smiling, hopped)*

important words in the story (e.g. *beautiful, castle*)

30

| 1 Read as a writer | → | 2 Make a plan | → | 3 Write |

Publishing your story

Remember who your story is for.

How are you going to share your story?

tell it

put it on a website

puppet show

make a book

Think about:
- illustrations
- blurb
- cover

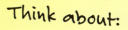

Adventure stories

What are adventure stories?

Everyone loves to read an exciting adventure story. In adventures all sorts of things could happen:

- ◎ **rescuing:** a princess, your best friend, a wealthy millionaire, a famous pop star, your dog…
- ◎ **finding treasure:** a strange box, jewels, a stolen painting, a secret invention…
- ◎ **surviving:** on a desert island, lost in a forest, trapped underground…
- ◎ **defeating a baddie:** a gang of robbers, a scientist who wants to rule the world…
- ◎ **finding something hidden:** a strange looking message, an old map, a secret tunnel…
- ◎ **a chase:** by a wild dog, a gang, a spy…

> Adventures are stories that could happen – but they're not always likely to happen.

Writer's checklist

Adventure stories

☐ Start with an **exciting idea** or **problem** to solve.

☐ Create one or two **characters** who solve problems and beat baddies by working together, or by using special skills.

☐ **Build the problem** up by putting in 'just in time' moments.

☐ Keep the reader **thinking disaster is round the corner.**

☐ End by having the main character(s) **solve the problem.**

Language low-down

Adventure stories often include:

- **exciting openings and endings** (e.g. *"Look out!" he cried);*
- **dramatic connectives** (e.g. *Suddenly, All at once);*
- **exclamations** (e.g. *"Oh no!");*
- **short sentences** (e.g. *They were trapped);*
- **questions** (e.g. *Who had taken it? And why?);*
- **powerful action verbs** (e.g. *leaped, struggled, screamed).*

Author interview

Alan MacDonald

I have written over forty books for children as well as scripts for TV series such as *The Tweenies.* I live in Nottingham with my wife, three children and a cat called Mojo who likes to sit on anything I am trying to read.

Where do you get your ideas?

From a notebook where I scribble ideas. Sometimes a title just pops into my head.

How do you decide which ideas to turn into stories?

A story idea has to stick with me for a while. It keeps buzzing in my head like a fly till I write it down.

How do you make your adventures exciting?

The excitement comes from caring about the characters in the story. You have to feel what they feel.

What do you do if you get stuck?

I leave the story for a while and go for a ride on my bike. The answer often comes to me!

What do you do after you've written your draft?

I print it out and scribble all over it making changes. I'll do this four or five times till I'm happy.

What are your five top tips for writers of adventure stories?

1. Start with something happening.
2. Tell us what the character is thinking and feeling.
3. Place them in some kind of danger.
4. Give the story a strong sense of place.
5. Have an air of mystery so we learn the truth as the story unfolds.

Adventure stories

Reading as a writer

Opening
- Introduces the main character(s).
- Grabs the reader's attention.

Build-up
- Builds up the excitement.

Climax
- The exciting bit of the story.
- Must have lots of action.

Resolution
- The end of the climax – the main character gets out of the difficult situation.

Ending
- Wraps up the story neatly.
- The main characters 'win'.

1 Read as a writer → 2 Make a plan → 3 Write

Adventure at Sandy Cove

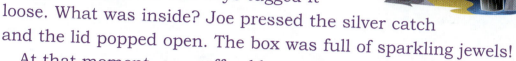

"Hey, what's this?" shouted Joe to Rahul. In the rock pool was a small, black box wrapped in plastic. The boys tugged it loose. What was inside? Joe pressed the silver catch and the lid popped open. The box was full of sparkling jewels!

At that moment, a scruffy old man shouted at the boys. His wolf-like dog barked menacingly. Joe snapped the lid down, picked up the box and the two boys began to scramble over the rocks. They slipped and struggled towards the cliffs.

"Quick! Let's hide in here," said Joe, rushing into a cave. It was dark and damp inside and they could hear water dripping. They felt their way further in and crouched behind a rock. Rahul's heart pounded like a drum.

Suddenly, the scruffy man appeared at the cave mouth. He shone a torch around. The light cast shadows on the cave wall. The children ducked down and kept as still as stone, but the dog could sense them. It padded closer and closer, growling threateningly. Rahul gripped Joe's arm. They could see its white teeth, smell its damp hair and feel its hot meaty breath.

Just then there was a distant shout.

"Here Dog!" hissed the man, roughly grabbing its collar. "Those boys have got away. Quick. After them!"

Joe and Rahul held their breath until they could hear the man and his dog stumbling back across the rocks. They waited for a long while before creeping out.

At first Mum didn't believe them. It was only when Joe opened the box that she decided to call the police. When the police arrived they told Mum that the big house up the road had been burgled only the night before. They had spent all day searching for a trace of the jewels. Their only clue had been the pawprints of a large dog. Joe shut his eyes. He could imagine the headlines: "PRICELESS JEWELS FOUND BY SCHOOLBOY DETECTIVES". And there was a reward too!

Planning to write your story

What is your story about?

◉ Finding treasure?

◉ Rescuing someone?

◉ Catching a baddie by setting a trap?

◉ Finding something hidden?

◉ A chase?

◉ A different adventure idea?

Who are your main characters?

◉ What are your characters **called**? Do they have **nicknames**? (E.g. *Tiger, Hammer, Rocket*.)

◉ What do they **look like**? What are they **wearing**? What's their **voice** like? (E.g. *sharp, low, gruff*.) How do they **move**? (E.g *limps, marches, stoops*?)

◉ What **sort of person** is your character? (E.g. *kind, clever, brave, mean*.)

◉ What are they **doing**?

◉ What's about to **happen**?

◉ What will your character **do/see/find**?

◉ How will they solve the **problem**?

brave

Joe — freckles

characters

thief

1 Read as a writer → **2** Make a plan → **3** Write

Safe settings

home

school

treehouse

Scary settings

deserted house

seaside cave

wasteland

Where is your story set?

- What's your setting **called**? *(E.g. Hangman's Forest, Rocky Pass, The Hut.)*

- What's the **weather** like? *(E.g. stormy, snowing, windy, sunny, raining.)*

- What **time of day** is it? *(E.g. early morning, dusk, midnight.)*

- What can you **see** and **hear**? *(E.g. wispy cobwebs, creaking floorboards, a door.)*

In adventure stories, try to start and end in a comfortable, safe place and have somewhere scary for the adventure.

Planning to write an adventure story

Make a story mountain

- On a story mountain the shape of the mountain shows the shape of the story.
- The most exciting part is the middle of the story.
- Use a new paragraph for each new part of your story.

Climax

They hide in a cave while the man searches for them.

Build-up

A man chases them.

Resolution

The man leaves. They wait and the run home.

Opening

Joe and Rahul find a box of jewels in a rock pool.

1 Read as a writer → **2** Make a plan → **3** Write

Writing your story

- Use your planning grid or story mountain to help you to remember what happened when.
- Jot down useful words and phrases on your planning grid.

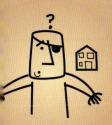

Top tips for writing

- Use your **story plan**.
- Don't have too much going on. Stick to the **main plot**.
- Keep your readers **interested** – don't solve the problem too quickly!
- Include a '**just in time**' moment.
- Use **short sentences** at the most exciting points.
- Use **powerful verbs** and **careful nouns**. (E.g. *The caretaker bellowed*, not *the man shouted.*)
- Show how characters **feel**. (E.g. *Her heart thudded. She screamed.*)
- Make sure that there is a **reason** for all of the events in the story.

Ending

Mum calls the police. They get reward!

Improving your story

How would you **improve** this story? Can you find the **mistakes**?

Ways to improve

- Don't use too many 'ands' – use full stops or a different connective instead.
- Use more powerful verbs.
- Use shorter sentences – this is more exciting.
- Use different sentence openings.

Mistakes

- Careless spelling
- Missing capital letters, full stops and question marks
- Paragraphs not used properly
- Missing speech marks
- Wrong tense used

Anything else?

Now do the *Writer's Mumble*.
Read your story aloud to yourself.

- Will your story opening grab the reader's attention?
- Will your story keep the reader on the edge of their seat?
- Is there anything you need to change?
- Have you rushed the ending?

1 Read as a writer ➡ **2 Make a plan** ➡ **3 Write**

Adventure at Sandy Cove

"Hey, what's this?" said Joe. He saw a box. The boys got it out. Joe pushed the catch and the lid opened. The box was full of jewels!

A man shouted at the boys and his dog barked and Joe closed the lid and picked up the box and the two boys went over the rocks and they went to the cliffs. Quick! Let's hide in here said Joe going into a cave. It was dark and wet and damp and dull inside and they could hear water. They went further in and got behind a rock. Rahul was frightened.

Then the man was in the cave. He got his torch. The children got down. The children kept still. The dog got closer to the children. He was scared. They could see the dogs teeth and smell its hair and feel its breath.

Then they heard a shout. Here Dog said the man, getting its collar Those boys have gone away. Quick. After them!" They held their breath and they could hear the man and his dog going back across the rocks and they waited before they went out.

Their mum didn't believe them and Joe opened the box and she called the police. The police got there and they told Mum that the house up the road had been robbed. They had spent all day looking for the jewels but the only clue had been the pawprints of a dog. Joe shut his eyes and imagined the newspaper saying: 'JEWELS FOUND BY BOY. And there was a reward too!

Improving your story

Make it better!

Try to improve your own story by:

- **varying sentence lengths** – short for suspense and long for description;
- using **powerful verbs** (e.g. *roared* not *said; stumbled* not *went);*
- including **descriptions** (e.g. *thunder boomed and lightning flashed in the dark sky);*
- including **alliteration** to make descriptions more memorable (e.g. *the rain roared and the lightning leapt);*
- showing how your characters **feel** (e.g. *his heart pounded like a drum).*

Language check

Have you used:

- the **past tense** all the way through?
- **dramatic connectives** (e.g. *Suddenly, At that moment*)?
- **time connectives** to tie the story together (e.g. *when, while, after*)?
- **place connectives** to show where things happen (e.g. *in the cave, over the hill*)?

Oops! Things to check for

- Sentence punctuation including exclamation marks
- Speech marks if you have used speech
- Missing words (it's easy to miss out *the* and *a*)
- Spelling

common words (e.g. *they, because, with*)

ing and *ed* words (e.g. *racing, gripped*)

important words in the story (e.g. *danger, suspicious*)

1 **Read as a writer** ➔ 2 **Make a plan** ➔ 3 **Write**

Publishing your story

Remember who your story is for.

How are you going to share your story?

make a book

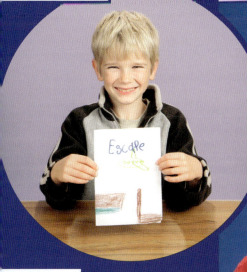

tell it

display it

film it

Think about:
- illustrations
- blurb
- cover

WRITER'S TOOL KIT

Using the Writer's Tool Kit

When you are writing, use these Tool Kit pages to help you.

In the Tool Kit are reminders about creating characters and settings as well as useful lists of connectives, verbs and adjectives.

It also includes reminders about punctuation and setting speech out. Use these after you have written to improve your writing.

Contents

Creating a character 47

Characters: adjective thesaurus 48

Characters: verb thesaurus 49

Creating a setting 50

Setting: adjective thesaurus 51

Setting: verb thesaurus 51

Paragraphs for planning 52

Story connectives bank 53

Punctuation

Punctuating sentences 54

Punctuating speech 55

Story writer's glossary 56

Some bits of the Tool Kit are colour coded. You will all be able to use the **green** examples; most of you will be able to use the **orange** examples, and some of you can use the **red** examples.

CREATING A CHARACTER

1 Choose a **name** (e.g. *Jake, Jo, Sandi*)

2 Would **a nickname** sound more interesting? (e.g. *Mags, Whistler, Baz*)

3 Describe one or two **details** so the reader can '**see**' your character (e.g. *freckled face, red jeans, scruffy trainers*)

4 How is your character **feeling**? (e.g. *angry, sad, lonely, excited, mean, jealous, brave, calm, silly, hungry, tired, happy*)

Remember: think about how your character feels. What would they **say** or **do**? Let's put two characters into the same position – meeting a gang in the park – and see what they do.

The brave character – *Jim stood on the path and waited with his arms folded. "Where do you think you are going?" he said sternly.*

The shy character – *Baz turned immediately and dashed back to the car. "There are some boys coming," he blurted out.*

Noun building

Who is your character?	– *a boy called Jake*
Add in description.	– *a tall, scruffy boy called Jake*
What is your character doing?	– *a tall, scruffy boy called Jake dashed*
Where is your character?	– *a tall, scruffy boy called Jake dashed down the road*

47

angry – bad-tempered, boiling, cross, fed up, fuming, furious, stormy.

bad – cruel, evil, foul, grotty, hideous, horrible, mean, naughty, rotten, sneaky, sour, terrible, vicious, villainous, wicked.

frightened – afraid, alarmed, fearful, ghostly, petrified, scared, spine-chilling, terrified, trembling.

happy – contented, delighted, glad, jolly, laughing, merry, thrilled.

nasty – disgusting, foul, horrible, horrid, mean, revolting, unkind.

nice – amazing, bright, charming, fantastic, generous, incredible, kind, pleasant, stunning, wonderful.

sad – depressed, gloomy, glum, lonely, miserable, moody, sorrowful.

weary – exhausted, footsore, shattered, tired, worn out.

Can you think of any more interesting adjectives or verbs?

Characters: verb thesaurus

cried – grizzled, howled, roared, screamed, screeched, shouted, sobbed, wailed, wept, whimpered, whined, whinged, yelled, yelped.

looked – examined, gaped at, gawped at, gazed, glanced, glimpsed, observed, peeped, peered, stared, viewed.

ran – bolted, dashed, galloped, hurried, hurtled, jogged, raced, rushed, scampered, scooted, scurried, scuttled, sped, sprinted, trotted.

said – babbled, bawled, bellowed, blurted, called, chatted, complained, cried, croaked, declared, gossiped, groaned, howled, moaned, mumbled, murmured, muttered, objected, pleaded, roared, screamed, screeched, shouted, shrieked, snapped, snarled, spoke, spilled the beans, squealed, stammered, uttered, wailed, whimpered, whined, whispered, yelled.

walked – ambled, crawled, crept, hiked, hobbled, limped, lurched, marched, paced, plodded, prowled, rambled, sauntered, scuttled, slinked, staggered, stalked, stepped, stomped, strode, strolled, stumbled, swaggered, tiptoed, toddled, tramped, trudged, waddled.

CREATING A SETTING

1 Decide where your story takes **place**.

2 Give your setting a special **name** (e.g. instead of *the house* use *Darkplace Hall*).

3 Describe the **weather** (e.g. *the storm rumbled*).

4 Describe the **time of day** (e.g. *it was late at night when …*).

5 Describe one or two **details**, so the reader can '**see**' your setting (e.g. *the window was grimy and cracked*).

6 Describe a **sound** to bring the setting alive (e.g. *something scratched at the door*).

7 Use **alliteration** to make descriptions memorable (e.g. *the frozen forest*).

Noun building

a) **a place**

Where are you?   – *The mountain*

What is it like?   – *The dark mountain*

Where is it?   – *The dark, distant mountain*

b) **description of a detail in the setting**

What can you see? – *The fence*

What is it like?   – *The metal fence*

Where is it?   – *The metal fence round the tunnel*

Setting: adjective thesaurus

beautiful – amazing, brilliant, charming, delightful, elegant, fascinating, glamorous, good-looking, gorgeous, handsome, lovely, pretty, spectacular, stunning, sweet.

big – colossal, enormous, gigantic, great, heavy, huge, hulking, immense, large, mammoth, mighty, mountainous, spacious, vast.

bright – blazing, dazzling, gleaming, glistening, glittering, glowing, shimmering, shiny, sparkling, sunny, twinkling.

cold – bitter, bleak, chilly, cool, crisp, freezing, frosty, frozen, icy, shivery, snowy, wintry.

dirty – dingy, dusty, filthy, grubby, messy, mucky, polluted, scruffy, shabby, stained.

hot – baking, boiling, burning, fiery, flaming, scalding, scorching.

little – baby, dinky, mini, minuscule, short, small, tiny, weeny.

wet – bedraggled, damp, drenched, dripping, soaked, soaking, watery.

Setting: verb thesaurus

made a noise – creaked, howled, roared, rustled, scratched, thundered, whispered.

moved – dashed, pushed, rustled, scurried, smashed, swayed, trickled.

Weather verbs

Wind can …   blow, roar, whistle

Thunder and lightning can …   crack, flash, light up, rumble, zigzag

Sun can …   bake, burn, glow, parch

Rain can …   drip, drizzle, pour, soak

Fog can …   drift, thicken

51

PARAGRAPHS FOR PLANNING

Prince leaves home

Travels into forest

Falls asleep under tree

Tree comes alive and grabs him

Mice free Prince by nibbling tree

Prince rewards mice

Suggested paragraph starter

- Once upon a time,
- Early one morning,

- After a long ride,
- Later that day,
- When he reached the forest,

- He was so tired that
- When the sun set,
- After his meal,

- Suddenly,
- To his horror,
- Before his breakfast,

- He was amazed to see
- Out of the corner of his eye,
- "Eek!" he screamed.

- At last,
- "I don't know how to thank you," he said.
- Back in his kingdom,

Reason for starting new paragraph

- Beginning of story

- Change of time
- Change of place

- Change of action
- Change of time

- Change of action
- Change of time

- Change of action
- Speech

- Change of time
- Speech
- Change of place

52

STORY CONNECTIVES BANK

Once upon a time,

One afternoon,

Suddenly,

… and … so … but

Then,

In the end,

One hot afternoon,

First,

Next,

After that,

Soon,

At that moment,

… and … so … but … because … if … when …

So

Just as

Finally,

Lastly,

Early/late one morning,

After a while,

Without warning,

Although

… and … so … but … because … if … when … until … who …

When

Just as

As soon as

In the end,

PUNCTUATION

Punctuation marks help your readers make sense of your story.

Punctuating sentences

Question mark to make the reader think	Full stop at the end of a sentence	Exclamation mark to show something exciting, surprising or funny
How do you count cows? 	 I don't know. 	Use a cow-culator! 

You can use commas in a description of character or setting.

He had a long cloak, shiny shoes and a red nose.

Inside there was a fire blazing, a red carpet and old paintings on the wall.

Punctuating speech

Important rules for writing speech include:

- **start a new line for each new speaker;**

- **put speech marks around the words the speaker says;**

- **use commas to show the end of the speech in speech marks, unless there is a question or an exclamation.**

Examples of dialogue:

"Look out!" Ted shouted. "Did you see that?"

"I think it was a dragon," replied Daisy.

Instead of said, why not try:

asked	called	moaned
shouted	yelled	whined
whispered	muttered	complained
	replied	exclaimed
		responded

The word you use instead of *said* can show us how the character is feeling. You can either add an **adverb** to the word *said*:

"I never wanted to fly," Tom said sadly.

"It's a wolf!" Poppy said suddenly.

or choose a better **verb** which shows us how the character is feeling:

"I never wanted to fly," Tom muttered.

"It's a wolf!" Poppy yelled.

55

STORY WRITER'S GLOSSARY

adjectives – Use these to add more information to a noun, (e.g. *the red car*).

adverbs – Use these to add more information to a verb, telling the reader 'how' (e.g. *slowly*), 'when' (e.g. *yesterday*) or 'where' (e.g. *upstairs)* things happened.

alliteration – A sound effect that makes words memorable. Words close to each other start with the same sound (e.g. *the curious, cunning clown crept carefully).*

connectives – These are joining words that link parts of a sentence (e.g. *and, so, but)* or link two sentences (e.g. *after, although, however).*

exclamation marks – Use after something short and punchy. Often this will be a command or warning (e.g. *"Stop!").*

nouns – These are naming words for people, places and things (e.g. *police, car, hat).*

prepositions – Words that show where something is (e.g. *under, above, below).*

question marks – Use a question mark at the end of a question (e.g. *"What was that?").*

speech marks – When you write down what people say, you need speech marks at the beginning and end of what they say (e.g. *"Watch out!").*

verbs – These are doing (e.g. *ran)*, being (e.g. *were)* or having (e.g. *had)* words.

The verb *to be*

I am, you are, it is, we are, they are.

I was, you were, it was, we were, they were.

Beware of writing *we was* – it should be *we were.*